Kevin Irie's third poetry collection ranges from Little Italy in Toronto to Italy itself, to explore the fusion of personal and historic memory and nationality within the context of growing up in multicultural Canada. In such a world, food and language can define identity or alter it, and an urban North American past can haunt contemporary Venice. A third generation Japanese-Canadian, he writes that

> *Memory is the country I hold*
> *as a citizen displaced*
> *by my time in the world.*

Also by Kevin Irie:

Burning the Dead
The Colour of Eden

Dinner at Madonna's

Kevin Irie

Frontenac House
Calgary, Alberta

Book design by EPIX Design.

National Library of Canada Cataloguing in Publication Data

Irie, Kevin, 1953-
Dinner at Madonna's / Kevin Irie.

Poems.
ISBN 0-9732380-0-3

I. Title.
PS8567.R46D56 2003 C811'.54
C2003-910036-7
PR9199.3.I685D56 2003

Frontenac House gratefully acknowledges the support of Canada Council for the Arts and The Alberta Foundation for the Arts for our publishing program.

Printed and bound in Canada.
Published by Frontenac House Ltd.
1138 Frontenac Avenue S.W.
Calgary, Alberta, T2T 1B6, Canada
Tel: 403-245-2491 Fax: 403-245-2380
editor@frontenachouse.com www.frontenachouse.com

1 2 3 4 5 6 7 8 9 07 06 05 04 03

in memory

Acknowledgements

Some of these poems previously appeared in the following publications:

Arc
The Antigonish Review
The Dalhousie Review
European Judaism (England)
Event
Grain
the Harpweaver
lichen
The Nashwaak Review
Pagitica
Queen's Quarterly
Rice Paper
The Toronto Review
Vallum

The poem "Tashme" won first prize in the 2000 Poetry Competition in *Rice Paper*.
"Entering Venice" won special mention for the 2002 Confederation Poets Prize selected by Douglas Lochhead for Arc.

Thanks to John Barton, Connie daSilva-Borges, Joan Harcourt.

Contents

Dinner at Madonna's

Old Men from Italy

They stand on College Street,
penned in by municipal pavement,
no *campo*, no *piazza* to carry their voices
back to the Old World.
Language, the sole import
that travels easily.

Memory is a shadow that follows them home,
a shadow falling from groves of olives,
chestnuts you can actually eat.
Look how their hands sweep the air
as if somehow they could banish the cold
and clear a space for the sun to shine
from that time
to this place.

Toronto Wine

The landscape clears the air each autumn
as leaves turn brown as the aged stained wood
in revered armoires storing vintage flasks.

Pale yellow crates of timber
splashed by the royal purple watermark
are stacked on sidewalks along Clinton, Grace Street,
pressed grapes like a fabric sample of wet crushed velvet.
Time makes its slow delivery of wine from house to house,
bottles in the dark of a monastic cell.

One sip and the palate is cleared
for bliss. Scent is a fragrance back to the past,
a fine catch of grapes at the end of the season
to bring back home,
to bring home back.

Memory, The Night Streetcar

The Carlton streetcar, west from downtown. Night ride home, after the movie, just before curfew. Young couples sitting side by side.

At Queen's Park, boarding, come legions of mothers up from Bay Street. Their night shift over, cleaning the offices. Their voices pitched against the silence of teens who recognize their parents' approach. Mothers whose sons and daughters ride home. The streetcar, suddenly the neighbourhood street, lit up for adult inspection. A church interior at late night mass. Each seat a pew where so-and-so's son and so-and-so's daughter share their communal despair together. The smiles and whispers of mothers staring. No wonder bourgeois life seems exotic for such adolescents. Mothers always home at midnight. Neighbours safe behind picture windows. Fathers rich enough to doze in their dens.

Here, parents and progeny disembark together. The mothers behind their young like a procession past families on porches, in darkness. Or judgement. *Banish the porch*, some budding architect notes in his mind. *Let him get his licence*, a daughter prays. Vows of various kinds are sworn in secret, awaiting future delivery. The streetcar heading further into the night, freedom a passenger with neither a curfew nor neighbour who knows it by name.

Letters Home

Your letters back home
were maps of your progress,
charting a course where children existed
to pass their exams, then marry and multiply.

You spoke of new cars like having more offspring,
as if success were the infant conceived with immigration,
a photo sent along with your words to drive your achievements
all the way home.

You failed to describe
the way your goals were routed like traffic
in other directions, those detours
common as dead end streets:

long hours, harsh weather,
small bills turning to larger debts,
the children rebellious.

Bad news never existed in print.
Your letters were brochures sent to family
who could only visit with you by mail,
guests of your word on paper alone.

There, a pen could hold your children to curfew,
paper could keep your household happy.

Fluent at last in New World content,
you hid dismay like a second language
you spoke only in private, at home.

Silence: the one who would always listen
and never talk back

in English.

A Winter Coat

She sulks to school in the same
winter coat as last year,
new buttons added to older wool,

fooling no one

though mother insists it's good enough.

Those words a weak stitch ripped in the playground.

In class, she hangs her coat on the lower hook, hidden
like that self who celebrates New Year's after the others,
her tongue a button she has learned to keep fastened.

English is a needle that can sew her
to this world, language a thread
she pulls into knots.

At Dufferin Mall, mother warns her
Look, don't touch,
those twin orders always fitted together,
like a button to a blouse.

In shops, clothes are stocked like food in a larder,
rack upon rack awaiting inspection,
the price tags hanging from sleeves like tongues

stuck out
to jeer
her passing.

Remembering the Milk Wagon

When did it happen,
what ordinary morning
did sound last travel
from the horse drawn wagon
clopping down Manning, Euclid Avenue,
the clink of milk bottles
set by a door on a street that seemed
no different that hour
than any we wake to find today,
unaware if this dawn
was the final one granted,
another day certain
to be someone's last?

The Drugstore Calendar

From the drugstores
of the Fifties, the Sixties,

there were women delivered
to hang in kitchens,

their photo posted
in workrooms, dens,

calendars sent each year
to promote the local store

and recruit desire:
pin-up girls in tight bathing suits,

vivid corsets of pinks and reds,
an arm brushing away shoulder length tresses,

a head tossed back,
reclining as if those locks

were a pillow
to swoon on in public,

their mouth like Snow White's
gasping for breath

as she moaned from the tug
of the witch's laces

squeezing her waist
like a measuring tape.

From under half-opened lids,
such women stared,

eye shadow: hue
of a swollen bruise,

one woman primed,
be it hottest July or the winter solstice,

her long legs tapering
into high heeled shoes

pointed at the tip
like a sharpened pencil,

as if such limbs
were wood after all,

to be whittled down
to almost nothing.

The English

Toronto streets were different countries
south of Bloor Street, Harbord, College,
each block a border manned by families where
language shifted from house to house,
so Ukrainians were stationed next to Italians posted
in a former Jewish neighbourhood
while untold English roamed to the north,
some minority occupying the rest of the city.
Mostly unseen. Little contact.

But who were they, the English?
We didn't know. They were a name,
the place we lived in, *English Canada*,
not French. Not Italian. Not Chinese.
They were the people who had our queen,
her face in profile like a Roman coin,
and Caesar was someone we studied as Shakespeare.
They were the ones who were here before us.
Always *the English* as a point of reference,
a standard of measurement no one questioned
any more than one would challenge
Imperial Units.
                    Learn English,
children were told.
English as a Second Language.
So the first won't hold you back.

The English were exotic.
Yorkshire Pudding
was a dish unknown.
Something English and vaguely odd,
lost in translation between dinner and dessert.

In high school, first names
were turned in with jumping jacks,
skipping ropes, knee socks,
the past put away like a childish thing
to grow up English.
Call me Mary. Call me Charlie.
Foreign vowels and diphthongs
were removed from mouths like baby teeth.

All this done before the term *ethnic*.
Just straight off the boat.

We laugh at that now, over Thai cuisine,
or in Portuguese restaurants,
in basement kitchens used by family, the way
the English have downstairs rec rooms;
dear *Maria* returned from being *Mary*,
George come back to *Giorgio* again.
English, a language as a foreign word
right here in Toronto, any city.

A joke we discuss now, in native accents,
in English,
that old friend at the table,
the only place
our words
feel at home.

The Old Neighbourhood

The people who moved in with your memory
have all moved on,

the future a residence
with no forwarding address.

The widows who pinned
their hopes and dollars

to the plaster Virgin
in the Easter Procession

are dead on the lips
of the newest neighbours

who live where her life
has passed into history.

Ripe backyard tomatoes
ripen best in the past,

and the nuns who strode down the street
in black raven wings

to swoop on the schoolyard,
fly from the doors of the Catholic school

that will close like the covers
of an old family Bible,

sacred, revered,
untouched.

A Tintoretto at the AGO

North January light.
Above the polished floor

smooth as an icy *campo*
in a cold Venetian winter,

the Tintoretto hangs,
stiff frozen tapestry.

Snow could not fall any whiter
than this pigment

carved into pillars
by an artist's brush

as Christ washes his disciples' feet,
unaware how centuries

have shipped him like cargo
to this New World,

docked the painting
like a vessel in Toronto.

What old tale is here,
smuggled on canvas?

My soul is no longer
an entry for God

or shelter for Satan.
I could kiss that Jesus

bowed before me
but not the cross that carries his death—

blunt dagger drawing its blood
from the spirit.

What Tintoretto painted excels:
red cloth smooth and glistening

as organs extracted,
still moist, in an autopsy.

A sacred relic by virtue of death.
Art is a corpse on public display.

Sunday at the Vatican

The red tapestry,
hung from the ledge,
flaps in the breeze
like a panting tongue
as he stands, so small,
in the window's darkness,
his white shape:
a lone tooth
in an ancient mouth.

A Wedding Party in Tuscany

Wedding, marriage, ceremony?
I ask some women as a party
descends from the Fiasole chapel.
I rummage through words like an index file
until a woman replies, *Esposa, si.*
Yes, I thought, *Esposa, spouse, espouse*,
a melody shifted to a different key.
A single lily
held by the bride:
                a trumpet
whose silence
becomes clear music
when accompanied
by meaning.

Entering Venice

She looks a sea Cybele, fresh from ocean,
Rising with her tiara of proud towers
At airy distance…
– Byron, *Childe Harold's Pilgrimage*

Spanning
the breadth,
the back of Venice:
graffiti scribbled across bare walls,
a gorgon's coil
writhing against the water,
slick tentacled creatures
caught in low tide

Sprayed ropes
scale Castello, Cannaregio;
green, pus yellow,
to tow the sight past walls
where a gangrenous
cut in a portal
marks a gash as welt and whip.

Hearts become serpents
swallowing their tails;
their purple, not royal, but bruised.
Damp worms, eels,
plucked from the ocean
that wrings them out
till they seep faint blood.

Here, words are vines
of an invasive species
borne by aerosol winds;

signature set as its own gaudy subject,
cheap paint
                    as netting,
lattice. Scar.

Not beauty
                but what defines it.

Venice:
a catch lashed in painted nets.

Each launch,
a finned creature
moving in
closer…

Touring the Doge's Palace

Our guide is the thread
we follow through this maze
of galleries, chambers,
ceilings rising to push us down smaller,
gilt coiled in carved ropes above us,
swags of gold
like piped yellow icing gone stale.

Tintoretto's *Paradise*,
large as a billboard,
hoards its side of the Great Council Hall.
No photos allowed, our guide reminds us,
her words our only souvenirs
as she draws us over the Bridge of Sighs,
lets us peer out its double windows,
live eyes behind a marble mask.

In the ducal prison,
she opens a door
like a giant book cover
to tell us the tale of Casanova,
of how he was held, escaped,
history the last
remaining tenant
to serve out its days
for the viewing public;

this palace:
a clock
stopped at that hour
when Venice kept time
for Europe.

Open Market

The sun,
round and white,
is an empty platter.
The Venice market spills beneath it,
ribbons of pasta
coiled into balls, tapeworms;
a bound soft fist
punching
the stomach.

What do you want?
Oil is thick phlegm
oozing behind glass,
while cheese opaque as candle wax
swells inside cellophane
a row of fat butts squatting on the shelf.

Here are dried beans rolling in their crates
like gravel, pebbles, spent bullets from the war
across the border.

The boats deliver catch like refugees,
the dead offered up for human inspection –
mouths, lungs,
slit throats, limbs,
eyes like nailheads hammered into flesh,
Plump cuttlefish soft
as severed bladders, their tentacle
entrails. A cool dead jelly
in human colours.

Here is a crab,
shelled prehistoric spider,
its back smooth as the market cobblestones
sprayed to wash off unwanted blood.
Newspaper wraps fish, the dead,
whose count is salt in seawater.

Venetian Glass

Once it's open for business,
the tourists are taken
into a show room

of ducal dimensions
where, locked behind cases,
are vases, vessels –

fantasy fired into glass.
The multiples of a singular craft
dividing attention.

Rows of shelves
like fashion runways
where glass is couture,

a fabric worked into
flounces and ruffles,
a Renaissance ruff

on a Modigliani neck.
Vases are sleeves of a Pucci gown.
A sleek glove rising

on a mannequin's arm.
A tray's curved handles
are straps on a dress.

Think a coral reef plundered,
a bed of anemones
in an aquarium tank,

round blown bowls like
clear gutted jellyfish,
handles for tentacles, stingers, prongs.

Colours strafed with darker hues
like horn tips stained
with gored crimson.

Glass beads bulging
like swollen slugs,
bubbled blisters –

an odd effect where
blood pools into beauty
if the wound is art.

It's just a trick.
Impress
to be purchased.

These small round jars
like chrome balloons inflated
yet open,

these goblets
in the shape of school bells
whose ringing means shattered.

These vases fashioned
into upended parasols on the scale
of infancy.

How they gleam together,
opaque or clear, one luminosity
shared in the other.

Green platters like melting lily pads,
pale plates like full moons
reflected on water.

Glass sculpted to be lit like a painting,
the glassblower's tongs:
his chisel and brush.

Glass pulled like taffy
to sweeten the taste
for a Venice confection

where *ghiaccio* ice
refuses to melt and *lattimo* milk
will never sour –

a feast served
not to be
touched.

Tourist

Walk through rooms
as if through a jungle

where carved beams
thick as anacondas

scaled in gold
rest coiled and poised

from leafy ceilings, ready to strike.
If only a chair

were free to sit on,
if only a wall could be touched

in rest. So much glitters,
crusted in gilt. *Midas was here!*

should be the text crimped
in Italian and English

on glass-covered cards
posted on stands

we hold between our hands
to steady ourselves

for yet another round
of silk and shimmer,

so much beauty hardened
into art.

Titian, Giotto, Veronese,
names are added up

like items on a bill
to convey their value before us.

We are children on a field trip
told not to touch,

to stay with the group,
dentures, chest hair notwithstanding.

When does one painting
blur into others,

the impressions of one room
vanish in the last?

We look at nudes in marble and oil
as we sweat under armpits,

not one body
on the scale of such art.

If only our interest
could equal the culture,

not think of where the toilets are located,
the souvenirs wait,

debate whether so-and-so
merits a postcard and stamp –

overseas at that.
If only we knew how much longer to go,

before the tour ends,
before the trip is over

and memory tells us we had a good time,
saw all the sights

we glance at like a watch.

Marble

I sat beneath the dome of the church
as if at the bottom of an empty well,

took out my guidebook
like a brick, Venice
being so weighted with history.

Light fell as ladders
high enough to climb
to examine the frescoes

where figures clung
to upper walls like bats,
their draped cloth furled wings.

I didn't know marble
could pack up moisture
like Monet storing his paints in a box.

But when I stood up, I felt it –
how stone was a brush
that used me for canvas,

the stain on my pants,
a kiss of the ass
where dampness left its signature.

Night

Venice at night
is an opera set where
the audience is allowed

to wander onstage,
like flecks
in the floodlights.

Night and voltage
mix to alchemize stone
to a shiny new alloy,

its luster: copper
on San Giorgione Maggiore,
a gold on San Marco

shot with silver,
a radiance that casts
the human into shadow.

Pigeons sleep under eaves
a row of grey hats
for conservative matrons

while tourists flutter through
the piazza below.
Pulled by their guide,

they ripple like a fringe
of a drawn stage curtain
off to the wings.

The sea plays a role
in this, of course –
defies the odds

to fuse water with fire,
forges reflections
of overhead lamps

into luminous lily pads
afloat on canals;
rocks the gondolas

along the quay
like rows of scimitars
slicing the water,

its transformation:
a brilliance
independent of light.

Venetian Marbled Paper

Think of gold like pollen
on water. Silver reduced
from metal to tint.

The Japanese art
of marbling paper
converted in Italy –

blank virgin sheets
baptized with colour,
daubed with oil,

lifted reborn
to singular glory
in multiple hues.

Paisleys arrayed
like book-pressed ferns,
peacock feathers.

Ripples of kerosene
ignited on pages left untouched,
a flicker of fire flamed

into art. Delicate
sheen or opaque
raindrops. The smallest

and most beautiful
washing hung up
in all of Venice.

Tintoretto's Abode

Beside the canal, its water
like a moving work in progress,

he lived in this house
in Cannaregio: Tintoretto,

the doorway closed,
a curtain down on a final act.

Peer into the ruin
as if at a canvas,

as if such timber
was the frame around the man

and the half moon
his palette donated to heaven.

The figures he painted
still hover on walls

in Dorsoduro,
San Marco, San Rocco.

They move among pillars, saints
and seraphim, imports

from the corners
of his imagination

to map a distance
only the brush can travel;

each stroke
the power within his hand

to summon the weather
beyond its season,

or raise up a Biblical life
presumed dead.

Here, where centuries press
decay into stone

like an artist applying
paint to canvas,

he has settled the city
with gods and cherubs,

though his body be dust,
his tombstone plain

as the canvas back
of a finished painting.

How many angels can dance
on the head of pin?

As many can hide
in an artist's brush.

God Creating the Animals

(The Galleria Accademia)

See how the artist
lights the canvas like kindling,
using God
as his central fire,
beams of light
the golden javelins
aimed for the backs of creatures below.

His brush is a match
igniting
live tissue;
the land beasts brown as seared meat,
gray doves in flight
like puffs of smoke
trapped against the sky's
blue tarpaulin.

Pigment
is the fuel
that keeps the image
lit for centuries,
sears the sides of flesh, feathers;
hooves like charred stumps,
claws like peeled tinder,

the earth
stirred thick
and heavy as smoke
on Tintoretto's
canvas.

Giorgione's The Tempest

What occurs
is the coupling
of water and trees
mated into one green hue,
dry blades of grass
like flicks of yellow lightning.
A woman nursing a child by a stream.
The city, a detail
set in the distance,
and a man set down
where no one can stop him,
who smiles at what
another might plunder:
a naked female,
unguarded, alone,
And what holds each,
right there on canvas,
is something almost
clear in the lightning,
or maybe the clouds,
if only they'd part –

words a poor brush
to render the silence
painted
so perfectly
in place.

The Plague Saint

It is you they prayed to
when it arrived –
cholera, death,
rats and fleas at home
in the cloths and silks of Venice,
port of plague,
death to the people
who sank to their knees
in chapels, the church,
its marble like ink spilt into cream,
the one fear spilling out
of them all.

Suffering. Agony.
The fearful and ill kneel in prayer,
their outstretched arms laid on the altar
like surrendered swords
while pain thrust into you,
arrows through the groin, lymph, throat, armpit,
each place the plague
could swell and enter.

Saint Sebastian, martyr,
helper of the sick –
in portrait after portrait,
your arms are tied at the wrist. Two bound stalks.
Your fingers, pale buds set to open,
Or shrivel.
So who did you save?

Titian pleaded for his life, his son.
Hope was a brush by which he thought
to paint a look of salvation
from your turned face,
be artist enough to summon
redemption. But only his Pieta
was left to survive.
Titian, his son, killed, gone.
The thousands of victims
just bristles on a brush
gathered together to paint plague's portrait,
a work in blood. Flesh: the canvas
that brings out its depth.

Mary Hunter, Patron

Mary Hunter,
long dead, gone,
no books on her life, no catalogue
of her collected works.
Edwardian wife, hostess,
her life the shadow that fell from another's,
her husband, his fortune
in Victorian mines.

Coal was the fuel that let her travel
to Italy, Venice, to rent Palazzo Barbaro,
its windows facing the Grand Canal, the Accademia Bridge,
a villa whose pedigree could be traced
all the way back to *The Wings Of The Dove*.
Where Henry James wrote *The Aspern Papers*.
His words. Her setting.

Her gift for generosity granted to artists,
the writers and painters
whose talent was the one place she could not visit.
Hospitality was the commission
granted. Art was the feast they served her.
She gathered guests like paints on a palette,
her home her canvas.
Edith Wharton. Sackville-West.
Rodin sculpted her head in bronze,
the gorgon touch of
immortal art.

John Singer Sargent.
His name, whispered as a lover,
mixing facts like oils
to render her portrait darker,
more compelling.

Her life encompassed them all like a frame,
the cover atop and beneath their books.
Knowing her presence fashioned their creation.
Without the hand.
The eye. The grasp.
To be that close so far from art.

Monet and Alice, she asked them to visit.
Let them discover the city,
pass days through the squares, galleries.
The nightly gondola trips like riding a dark swan
even as Monet's inspiration took off into flight.
Canvas, sables, tubes –
the bricks and mortar for Monet to construct his own Venice.

Then evenings. Moored gondolas
tied to the *pali*, those Venetian pilings
like tall brushes resting in water once the day's
work is done and it is time for a party.
Her parties. The palazzo aglow,
drapes like illuminated manuscripts.
Music from the grand piano
set against the adagio of waves.
Chandeliers lit, candles like brush tips dipped in fire.
Yes, here was status, prestige.
To be in such circles. Hostess and artists.

In the seeking, she was there –
Mary Hunter,
unwritten.
Her life, the reason Monet painted Venice.

Her place, that of paper before the words.
Not the picture painted
but the room
that held it. The patron in shadow
behind the artist, watching
what she could not see

for herself.

Monet in Venice

Imagine Monet at sixty-eight,
his first trip to Venice,
so late into life,
to find all he loved not yet all uncovered –
water and light renewed by this city,
a fresh source
never tapped before.

Despite Giverny,
the Seine. The Thames.
Now Venice. The Ducal Palace.
Palazzo Dario, Contarini.
The distant dome of Santa Maria della Salute,
a pink water lily
closed at dusk.

Monet, dazzled by how sun covered the city
as if walls were canvas brushed by light.
Furious with the gondolier
unable to find
exactly where they had anchored before
so he could finish his sketch before the sun retreats,
its distance dividing the hour from art.

Each day of rain meant time lost,
peering from the window
as Monet waited for light,
a subject for its monarch,
impatient for his hands to take his brushes like oars
along the Grand Canal,
to San Giorgione Maggiore,
the Palazzo Mula,
to make the canvas a tinted pane
where paint is afternoon sun through glass,
before rheumatism turns his fingers to
wooden brushes he cannot bend,

before the easel becomes a scaffold
where inspiration hangs dead.

Like paint stains under fingernails,
he cannot be rid of worries on health, age,
his fading sight.

To see the world as a pond underwater.

What a shame I didn't come here when I was a younger man,
when I was full of daring!
he wrote in December,
an old man letting the artist be drawn
to accept the challenge of Venice.
If the sky is a work of God signed by Turner,
then Monet will paint in its light.

Monet, seated outside in borrowed furs against wind
so cold skin tears, oozes blood,
crimson squeezed from a seam in a tube,
the chill on his fingers
like paint coating his brushes.

Or warm inside a rented funeral gondola,
its glass cabin his smallest studio,
crammed with sketch pads, canvas,
oil tubes spread like silver catch, bait;
his figure seen through the reflected pane,
immersed in his element,

one hand grasping the brush like a wand,
the other his palette,
its daubs of paint:
new buds atop the pond at Giverny,

while Venice floats before him like a raft of water lilies.

Ghosts

guests (if we imagine them) come some
distance for the meal…
– Steven Heighton

Near the Ponte dei Pugni,
just short of the *campo*,

I order dinner
at an outdoor table,

trusting my luck
more than my language

to find I am given
a first course of – what? –

looks like dried squid, shredded to laces,
Japanese food

heaped on the platter
and no one around

for me to comment that I never *was*
crazy about such food in the first place.

What of the dish the waiter described
to the couple one table over,

his words a small serving
of the feast before them:

lasagna in butter sauce
layered with zucchini?

What of the fork and knife,
plebian scepters

of Western rule
in an Eastern household?

No *shoyu*,
but wine at each table;

a carafe, a bottle,
the hue of dusk canals.

I could pass my order
to the ghost of my grandmother

who would never have dreamt
of visiting Venice,

share it with a late uncle
who wanted to see Europe

as long as he still had
his chopsticks and rice.

Among lace curtains woven in Burano
and this darkening *campo*,

its gelato shop
bright as a midway stall,

I imagine them sitting here –
family, lost, watching me eat:

grandmother, uncle,
faint whisper of the Japanese

I have never understood –
ghosts at my table finding their place

as memory leads me
to mine.

Mirror Image

Tower to smoke stack,
stucco to steel,
Venice faces
industrial Mestre
like Dorian Gray
his mirror.

On Death in Venice

Youth over age. The familiar story.
The Venice hotel. The beautiful boy.
The author, Aschenbach.
To speak as if he were a real figure,
who lived only on Thomas Mann's pages, a self
that came out when the author emerged.

Though a Tadzio was real enough,
a Polish boy in a sailor suit, locks,
A round straw hat like a woven halo.
Who played on the beach at the Hotel Des Bains, the Lido.
Sand on the skin like gold powder.
The froth of the Adriatic around his thighs,
a ring of white blossoms.

Umbrellas, cabanas,
yellow sand along the beach.
The long thin Lido sandbar,
a streamer rippling along the sea
as the author writhed,
his face a mask where desire peered out
from the man in want, the person so different
inside this other.

The starched collar, Brecht called him, arch-enemy.
Not knowing.
Though Katia's memoirs
pressed the youth like a rose between pages
where she could preserve
her wifely decorum.

Wherever they travelled, though,
did she fear, remember,
looking for a Tadzio to step from a beach,
out of a lobby, a German café,
to enter her life the way plague entered Venice?

In truth, no one died,
kissed, was kissed,
nothing happened between them.
Mann kept his place as a married author.
The boy to his family.
Each left, parted.
It was only back in their separate homes that
Mann could lay Tadzio out on the page as if on a bed
and still, reticent,
undress
himself.

To imagine a body in words.
Young lips, limbs, each part of him
prodded open on paper.
To read the body as a smuggled book under the covers.
Moments that linger for years in the mind.
All the stronger for having let go.

That spring took twelve months
to deliver. To write it down.
The beach, the Lido.
The look of a stranger.
A Gustave born from Mahler's death,
a man past fifty, his life distinguished as a medal
on the chest
of a boy.

Nothing is invented, he wrote of his story.
The hotel promenade with its tables, white linens,
the starched iron presence of hotel clientele,
a tablecloth laid over coarseness beneath.
Discretion and manners used
like the hankies and pomanders
the courtiers at Versailles kept close at hand
to deal with human rot.
Plague as desire, covered up.

Aschenbach roaming Venice to seek an answer.
To ferret out one truth
denying another.

Aschenbach,
wandering the lanes of Venice,
the sting and smell of its back alleys.
It took Mann a year to get that stench from his nostrils.

To write of the rogue gondolier.
The aged queen with his hair, rouge.
The mirror that presented
itself to the man
who saw what the boy could become
to his dignity.
Grotesque. A plague.

And the boy there on the beach,
hand on his hip,
looking. Knowing
he was wanted, a power
carried in the body for the body.
That power whose only source was the body.
A weapon wielded
without any training.

And the thousands of words to bring him down.

Campo del Ghetto Nuovo

To remember is a kind of hope
– Yehuda Amichai

History
does not charge
admission to this *campo*
where death
conscripted
its ranks for the camps,
where no church towers
toll for the lost,
an island apart
on city maps,
the canal around it
a slim blue necklace
across a throat,
a loose drawstring on a money pouch.

Ghetto,
a term first cast here
from foundry cinders,
Italian smelted
to forge a word
strong enough
to hold an entire race;

a word like a lock and a gate around a people.

A word like a broom
to sweep up Jews
into a corner
around the world.

Here, history falls
as a shadow from
buildings rising floor above floor,

the old law forbidding Jews to move elsewhere,
so they built upwards,
opened the sky
like plots of earth,

windows so high
that shutters were hinges,
joined on one side
to ghetto walls,
the other fastened to heaven.

*

The *campo* is empty,
deserted in sunlight.

It is the quiet of a sabbath
or an occupation.

In afternoon light,
what ghosts still mourn

for Giuseppe Josa, suicide
of the Nazi roundup,

the soldiers' grip
on captive shoulders

like hinges clamped on ghetto gates.
Also removed.

Where are the synagogues
hidden in the square,

their rounded windows,
like backs bowed in prayer

while the sun remains
at its usual post

patrolling the rooftops,
a white glint aimed

at the space below
where tourists now enter,

heads lowered,
silent,

to open their guides
like prayer books.

*

In mid-afternoon
at the Venetian ghetto,

centuries change several times
in the course of a stroll.

Washing hangs strung
across terraces,

window to window,
each a wet canvas

drying its portrait
of daily life.

In the *Campo del Ghetto Nuovo*,
shadows lie on their backs

to gaze up at the heights
from where they have fallen,

twin windows aloft
in the upper storeys

like tablets raised
in a prophet's hands.

Touched by sunlight,
shutters open or close

by the *Casa di Riposo*
where a few old men still engage in banter

against the silence
of those driven off,

the living here
now smaller in number

than leaves on the few last
trees in the *campo*,

where the dark
bronze plaques

of the Holocaust Memorial
are set into brick,

still warm to the touch.

*

Three lions of Judah
carved from rock

yellow as August grass
in drought

survey the *Campo del Ghetto Nuovo*,
encircle the well where

stone holds drink
as wheat holds bread.

Three wells to
quench the Jewish Ghetto,

three altars
raised to the power of thirst.

Metal lids shut them shut as urns,
water trapped in

untapped darkness, no Moses
to raise their taste

to the light. Those lids
could be doors

of an oven closing.
The graffiti

scarring the wall
a tattoo.

A hundred lives more
could be telling their stories

under the shade trees
counting the dead

among the scattered leaves
in the *campo*

where one footstep sounds
for those silenced before it.

An old woman
crosses the square alone,

drags her shadow behind
like a train.

What is left in Venice
after Byron, Shelley, Ruskin, Pound?

What hasn't been done?
somebody asked.

The point. Exactly,
at this mark in the century.

What hasn't been done?

The Back Canals of Venice

This city's rags
are its bricks and plaster.

Wet sheets hang
from building to building,

a smile of bleached teeth
in a rotting mouth,

stucco brittle as
chipped enamel

as time works
on death's commission.

Yet this Sunday morning,
men push a new washer and dryer

through an open door
like placing new crowns for a waiting mouth,

a small procedure
applied to Venice

to keep the patient going.

Street Soccer

Down *Calle Del Traghetto*, a Venetian street
bare as a Toronto laneway,

four boys play soccer.
Their legs thrash at the ball

like hockey sticks swinging
to free a puck.

Their yelps are the cheer
of a stadium audience.

I wait as if given a chance
to be called to the game.

Amid their shouts
I hear my silence

telling me to listen
to what it hears –

for what is the game
but my own childhood,

and when a woman leans from an upper window
to call the boys in,

I too, look up,
half expecting to see

my dead mother
speaking in fluent Italian,

though only a stranger
calls to her children

as memory calls
to me.

Cannaregio

They practise together,
stroke by stroke,

the small son
towed by his father's wishes

as they stand in the barge
cresting the water,

vessel and canal
like car and roadway.

The license
is his father's hands.

Papa, papa! he shouts
as they glide

back and forth,
his father's words

now short, now long
tugging him, easing him

along the canal, the long poles
pushing away

whatever years
have risen between them.

Dinner at Madonna's

Surely, the world over,
there is a table like this
in some city, village, camp, canteen:
travellers seated together for dinner,
Let's Go, Lonely Planet, Eyewitness, The Rough Guide, Fodor's, placed atop the table, page corners folded,
as sights are compared, dismissed, recommended,
what bus to take, what times are best.

Tonight, it is Venice and *Alla Madonna*,
seafood fare just past the Rialto,
as a heavy May rain pours outside,
surges beneath the shut French windows.
Across the carpet, waiters drag mops
like skewered anemones at the end of spears.

It's Venice, becomes the common consensus
as purses on floors are pulled up like catch
and jackets slung low over backs of chairs
are tugged to the safety of higher ground.

The English menu passes from person to person,
a white winged creature fluttering down the table,
Adriatic fish the topic for talk,
as is the weather. The German couple, worried,
their Lido hotel only reached by ferry.
The Californian who had to give up on Rome,
its roads too fast. And it was raining there as well.

And Canada – spoken as a destination, memory.
How strange to hear my country
as a place on a postcard,
odd to hear home as a site to explore.

The English boy awed by the size of Algonquin, Niagara
Falls.
The Americans in love with Vancouver, B.C.,
Toronto's streets, old Quebec.
They talk until my country is a foreign word
even in its native tongue;
a new taste added to my own palate
even before our orders arrive
with *polenta, risotto*, cuttlefish ink,
enquiries as to *how is your serving?...*
English spiced with differing accents,
including mine, served to guests up and down the table
with talk of rainstorms, emptied streets,

my thoughts still full of Canada, country,
of travelling abroad
to find parts of home
in places where it never stood.

A Canadian in Venice

identity
something too huge and simple
for us to see
– Margaret Atwood

My childhood tells me
these are not its streets

though I hear it speak
in its many voices –

the clatter of dishes
through open windows,

chairs scraping against bare floors
like forks against platters,

the staccato burst
of greetings, kisses,

as doors open to women in black,
men in white shirts,

welcoming their children
and their children's children,

a family gathering
for one more Sunday.

Above me,
an opened bottle of wine

wafts its scent
like a secular incense

issued from a window
as I savour the aroma

of basil and tomato
simmering into stronger taste.

It is May in Venice
and I follow my guidebook

along *fondamente*
wider than College Street,

past gondolas
like ornate canoes,

a man walking further on
into childhood,

surprised to find his past
at this address

among the walkways
of Tintoretto's abode,

each sense a migrant
as memory provides

the documentation
allowing free passage

to discover Toronto
at home in the world

as the world is home
in Toronto.

Geraniums, Concord Avenue

Memory is possession,
and what is my own but
these geraniums blooming
in a Toronto window,

kin to those I recall in Venice,
their floral reds and pinks in challenge
against that city's domestic grey.

Now, each leaf is a ticket back,
my passage booked by a single glance.
Each red petal a tongue to proffer *return*;
the soft wax seal of an invitation.

Home, but not settled,
my life is a document
named for planting
in government files.

Memory is the country I hold
as a citizen displaced
by my time in the world.

In Passing

They're all dying, my uncle
tells me at the latest funeral,
the service in English, Japanese
food served at the home

where the neighbours ask
if the fish in the sushi is *really* raw,
and how do you eat it,
and does it taste – fishy?

The egg salad sandwiches chosen instead.

The *Issei*,
the oldest,
the first generation of immigrants,
most widows, nearing a century.

We rise,
give them a place to sit,
bring them sushi, rice bags,
a cup of green tea
as they peel off white gloves,
place black handbags by the side of the chair,
adjust their rimmed hats one more time
while the talk twists in and out of their hearing.

English is the stranger
who took their children away
from them years and years ago.

There are bean cakes,
coffee cake, side by side;

always the taste of one odd word or another
sticking to the tongue.

Eventually,
you learn to chew and swallow

or else
stay hungry.

On Race

Chinese bugs, my family knew,
were what separated *us* from *them*.

Chinese bugs, like fleas
in the blanket, nits in the carpet,

imported from China
in immigrant clothing,

thriving in Chinatown,
among the dens.

My maternal aunt still recoils
at the memory of seeing

their chopsticks dipped
into a communal pot,

how she politely declined
the offer of dinner,

yet feeds off that incident
fifty years later.

Another remembers
rice in a Chinese café,

where she saw how
the small mounds of hot grains on top

hid an old portion
in the bowl below it.

She didn't say anything,
but ate it quietly, confirmed

that the family's whispers
were right.

The family wouldn't be tricked
by the passing resemblance

of black hair, brown eyes,
yellow skin.

The whites thought them
templates of one common target,

tugged their Caucasian eyes
into slits.

But my family *knew*
the Chinese were different.

Just how much,
my family discovered

during internment,
the Second World War;

the Chinese walking free
in downtown Vancouver;

my family now
the visible aliens

in Slocan, Lemon Creek,
New Denver. The old mining towns.

White people's bugs,
my family discovered,

they were everywhere then,
all over the place…

Tashme

Tashme was the name of an internment camp for Japanese-Canadians during World War Two. Located 14 miles from Hope, British Columbia, it was surrounded by the Cascade Mountain Range.

Lay the wood
in the fireplace now.
Ignite those feelings
smoldering still from the memory of Tashme,
that very first winter.

Memory holds to the site of those homes,
uniform rows of wooden shacks,
government timber
shipped inland
abruptly
as you,
                    those upright
generations
cut.

Cabin walls beaded
with condensation, blankets
damp as if fevered,
the few books moist as those logs out back,
the wood that was green,
too wet,
not cured,
that gave little warmth
when placed in the stove
but just enough light to offer a glimpse
of how hard the winter ahead would be.

Remember how children wept from the cold
while grown-ups whispered, *It can't be helped*,
their words: kindling
lit in a blizzard,
wood's weak voice
in the family stove
where the wet fuel popped and sizzled flat.

Remember the evenings bolted inside,
where the household banter
said you were safe,
how even the clang of an empty kettle
could jar a memory of a kitchen on Powell Street,
how one plate carried
the weight of home,
how hands washed rice
like surf rolling gravel
while mother and father
presided at meals
and neighbours on the other side of the wall
bickered about the cold, the law.
Their voice was everything
your parents would not speak.

But you speak it now,
to your children, theirs,
though Tashme is almost a word snuffed out,
a site in the Cascades
cleared off maps
along with Bayfarm, Popoff, Sandon;
memory solid as the ice
that clamped your shoes to the floor by morning,
sharper than the memory
of home on the coast.

A memory
cured and dried as timber,
a funeral pyre.

Your mother and father both gone now.

And Tashme,

never warm enough in winter,

still can sear

and burn.

At the Table

Perhaps we are what we remember we ate
– Ken Babstock

Toronto evenings. At family dinners,
it was always the same:

clear bottles of *shoyu* on white linen alongside
the western
salt and pepper.

Kosher dills and Japanese radish.

Forks for the children.

Salmon, fresh
from the coast, gift
from a visitor in from BC,
grown-ups exclaiming
how nothing compared to coho,
sockeye, caught the same day,
setting the locale for the conversation that surface
at night –

the stories that were passed along with the chow mein,
brown rice, tempura.

Food was an offering
to coax the past back to the table,

to tell the stories of Slocan, New Denver,
the War.

Those small bitter servings of words for the young
who had only tasted life in Toronto.

*

Someone would mention the Mounties, their order to pack. A life's possessions to weigh 150 pounds. To report to the station. Ready to leave. Not knowing where. How long.
Winter clothes crammed like contraband. A bag of rice carried like a doll by a child.

*

That story,
told so often,
grown-ups always
feeding that memory
while children squirmed,
preferring instead the shrimp, roe herring eggs
like tiny white beads
sewn onto soaked dark bands of leather.

Tofu,
small floating bergs in cold water.

Beef teriyaki
served hot from the skillet.

*

But slices of beef invited back poor Mrs. M. and her infamous cow, the one she tried to sell off. A local, she walked by the camps in search of a buyer, tugging a beast that bore its sickness like a bell clanging around its slack neck until one day the cow just vanished, Mrs. M. walking again, alone, asking if anyone wanted to buy fresh meat.

*

All this served up in kitchens at night,
dining room tables, adults unaware
of how they'd sit up,
pull in their chairs
as they placed each friend
like a pin on a map.

Who was in Slocan?

Who was in New Denver?

And the young would groan
at *those* stories again,
tales that served
as surrogate sermons
on the easy life in Toronto.

The past
was a pill to be swallowed
so they could grow upright,
no oats rolled into the rice,

no Mounties knocking at the door.

They kept us where they kept the cattle!
In Hastings Park. The livestock stalls.
Those words singeing the tongue like radish, hot mustard.

An adult's acquired taste
for bitterness.

*

Fiddleheads too, bitter at first. To them. But plentiful in British Columbia, growing out back in the woods by Slocan. Source of greens each spring. How the grown-ups laughed years later when newspapers reported that fiddlehead greens were served at a state dinner in Ottawa.
Haute Canadiana.
No one here eating them for years,
for decades.

*

Then dishes were cleared
along with the past
to make way for Japanese tea,
black coffee,
cakes and pies that summoned
the need for forks for the grown-ups.

Apple pie. Lemon meringue.
Sponge cake. Homemade.
Processed white sugar
to cut the taste of Japan in the mouth.

Children released
to the living room, TV,
to trade hockey cards with all the fervour
their parents swapped tales of Lemon Creek and Tashme.

*

The evening over,
all talk of camps put away.
stored like linen or family china
to be taken out at future gatherings,
along with the chopsticks,
the bowls for *miso*,
as much a regular part of the diet
as the salt and *shoyu* set on the table,
present together at every meal
so no one forgot
its taste.

Kevin Irie was born and lives in Toronto. His poetry has been published in periodicals and anthologies in Canada, the United States, Australia and England, and has been translated into Spanish and Japanese. He won first prize in the 2000 poetry competition in Rice Paper for the poem "Tashme". He is also the author of two previous books of poetry, *Burning the Dead* and *The Colour of Eden* a finalist for the City of Toronto Book Award.

Burning the Dead
"...an accomplished and finely chiselled suite of lyric and serial narrative poems" – Richard Stevenson, *Canadian Literature*

The Colour of Eden
"...a beautiful second book of poems" – Libby Scheier, *The Toronto Star*,